D1473075

ACKNOWLEDGEMENTS

These quotations were gathered lovingly but unscientifically over several years and/or were contributed by many friends or acquaintances. Some arrived—and survived in our files—on scraps of paper and may therefore be imperfectly worded or attributed. To the authors, contributors and original sources, our thanks, and where appropriate, our apologies. –The Editors

CREDITS

Written by Dan Zadra and Kobi Yamada

Designed by Sarah Forster

ISBN: 978-1-932319-87-3

1st Printing (rev). 10K 10 09   Printed with soy ink in China

WHAT ARE
LITTLE GIRLS
MADE OF?

WRITTEN BY *Dan Zadra and Kobi Yamada*
DESIGNED BY *Sarah Forster*

COMPENDIUM™
INCORPORATED

THANK HEAVEN FOR
LITTLE GIRLS.

~Gigi

WHAT ARE LITTLE GIRLS MADE OF?

SUGAR & SPICE
& EVERYTHING...

FUN & PLAYFUL...

AND
BRIGHT

&

HOPEFUL...

& THOUGHTFUL & CARING...

& VIBRANT
& ALIVE...

and

PERCEPTIVE

&AWARE...

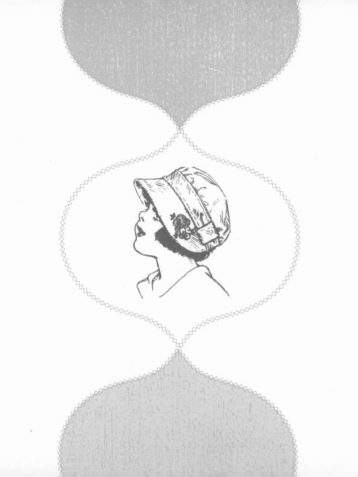

&STRONG

&TENDER...

& Sentimental

& Romantic...

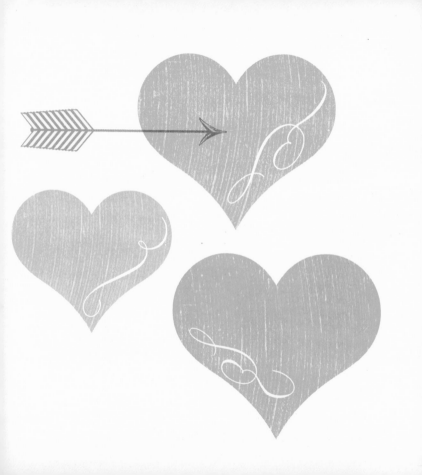

and INTELLIGENT
& CREATIVE...

AND WISE

and INTUITIVE...

 SPONTANEOUS

NATURAL...

& CONFIDENT

& DARING...

&TALENTED

&SKILLFUL...

AND GRACIOUS

and FORGIVING...

AND RESOURCEFUL

and RESILIENT...

&
PASSIONATE

&
LOVING...

&POSITIVE

&INSPIRING...

...& **ALL THINGS**
GOOD IN THE WORLD.

THAT'S WHAT LITTLE GIRLS ARE MADE OF.